THE COAST OF
MASSACHUSETTS

THE COAST OF MASSACHUSETTS

Photography by
Wayne Barrett and Anne MacKay

Introduction by
Anthony Bailey

SKYLINE
PRESS

ACKNOWLEDGEMENTS

*Our special thanks are due to
Ralph and Marlene Johansen, who made
Boston one of our favorite cities, to the
Reverend Way of Old North Church, Boston,
to the Peabody Museum of Salem,
to the 'Plimoth Plantation',
to Bill Carmen of the Hyannis Melody Tent,
to the Boston Art Commission, and to all who
assisted us in the photography for this book.*

WAYNE BARRETT and ANNE MACKAY

Designed by Fortunato Aglialoro

Produced by Roger Boulton Publishing Services, Toronto

© 1984 Oxford University Press (Canadian Branch)
SKYLINE PRESS is a registered imprint of Oxford University Press

ISBN 0-19-540611-7
1 2 3 4 – 7 6 5 4

Printed in Hong Kong by Scanner Art Services, Inc., Toronto

INTRODUCTION

For me this coast is a collage of impressions gained partly from the land and partly from the sea. But the single picture that comes most vividly to mind is one got a few years ago, from the third element, air—from a jumbo jet sweeping in from Europe at twenty some thousand feet on a summer day of absolute clarity. There below were the bays and capes and islands; green wooded headlands, grey rocks, bleached sand, and the frozen white fringe of surf edging the expansive blue of the sea. There was the whole bended arm of Cape Cod, looking more resolute than it does on a map as it defends the shores and waters behind it. There was nature's work, the drumlins and moraine that form the detritus of the last ice age, brilliantly beautiful, and with—apart from a few mainroad markings—very little of man's overlay apparent; even the constant pink-grey megalopolitan band of smog was well inshore. From up there one could follow the nooks and crannies of the coast and imagine the way the Indians traced its outline for Samuel de Champlain, as he stood on a beach at Cape Ann in 1605, using Champlain's crayon to show the French explorer the shape of Massachusetts Bay, and placing pebbles to indicate the whereabouts of their tribes. 'All along the shore there is a great deal of land cleared up and planted with Indian corn,' the Frenchman wrote. 'The country is very pleasant and agreeable, and there is no lack of fine trees.'

The coast of Massachusetts has never lacked a good press. Bartholomew Gosnold, three years earlier, had felt compelled to change the name of a 'mightie headland' from Shoal Hope when the quantities of codfish his men caught became an embarrassment. Henry Hudson reported on Cape Cod in 1609: 'The land is very sweet.' The news of prodigious fishing brought Captain John Smith in 1614, mapping the coastline, giving names to places and landmarks (most of which stuck), trading for furs, catching fish, and writing a report on the timber and many 'excellent good Harbours' to be found. He enjoyed these shores: 'And surely by reason of those sandy Cliffes and Cliffes of rock, both of which we saw so planted with Gardens and Corne fields, and so well inhabited with a goodly, strong and well proportioned People, besides the greatnesse of the Timber growing on them, the greatnesse of the Fish, and the moderate temper of the Ayre . . . . who can but approve this a most excellent Place, both for Health and Fertility?' It would be a fine place for a colony, he thought. 'Here every man may be master and owner of his owne Labour and Land.' Smith lauded—using the name in English for the first time—'the Countrie of the Massachusetts, which is the Paradise of all those parts.' His report made an impression back home in England, and probably had an effect in inducing the Pilgrims to try their luck in the New World—though when, after a month of reconnoitring Cape Cod, they reached their final harbor of Plymouth, they don't seem to have realized that Smith and other explorers had been there before them. Perhaps this isn't unusual. A coast remains in many ways personal—the sum of the landfalls we each make upon it.

And yet there's a common need to visit those places where earlier travellers landed and settled. Massachusetts is comparatively strong on claims to 'the oldest', 'the earliest', 'the first in North America'; and though the rock at Plymouth is now rather grandiloquently colonnaded, it provides a focus for the respect and curiosity we feel for those who came for a freer and more hopeful life—facing in the process the sea's perils, and privation and disease on shore—and who continued to come for several hundred years. The nautical dangers were often greatest in the moments of closing with the coast. Thoreau, on his way to Cape Cod for a walking trip in 1849, turned aside to visit the beach at Cohasset where an immigrant ship from Ireland had just been wrecked, with the loss of 145 lives. As I stand in line at Customs at Logan airport, I try to calm my impatience with recollections of the greater difficulties that faced our predecessors coming to these shores.

If John Smith were to visit the coast today, he would probably note its continued prosperity—and some of the effects of our fertility. The coast—for example near Lynn and the top end of Buzzard's Bay—is also strip-development, seedy roadsides littered with gas stations, fast-food merchandisers, basket shops, and asbestos-shingled motel cottages. Cape Cod strikes one recent visiting writer (whose equanimity may have been shattered by Massachusetts driving habits) as 'a summer jungle.' The summer air on the roads of Martha's Vineyard is filled with the staccato racket of mopeds, and the hospitals are filled with riders who have come off them, the shipwrecked of our time. Although many lighthouses remain, white sentinels above the cliffs and rocks, other landmarks have changed; instead of signal poles and beacons, there are city skylines, oil refineries, microwave towers, radar domes, and water tanks—that at Provincetown painted *eau de nil* green. On the coast where corn was grown and men went fishing, whaling, trading with China (and built ships for those purposes), the leading economic activity is tourism; and many of the tourists, liking what they see, want to stay. So, along the coast, the cohesion of communities is threatened by rapid expansion and change. The conflict is bumper-sticker fierce between those who want to keep the situation as it was when *they* arrived and those who want to make a living out of the newcomers' demands for living room. On the Cape and the larger islands the pressures of second-home development provoke legislation and zoning ordinances; meanwhile condominiums rise, and 'Private—Keep Off' signs flourish. Some who are landowners on a grand scale try to stay out of the public view—like the fortunate Forbes family on Naushon, in the Elizabeth Islands, hoping that the thrust of the twentieth century doesn't present them with a Hobson's choice of

selling out for many millions their carefully preserved haven of ancient trees and carless tracks fit for horses and deer; the old coast. The tension is great—as it was for the Indians and first settlers—between those who are in possession and want to conserve the pleasures of the coast and those who come to partake more recently and perhaps transiently of those pleasures, and in doing so seem to create a demand for tourist services, for aquariums and replica colonial villages.

However—for those who avoid the main highways in midsummer, walk the further strands, and cruise by boat into the smaller harbors and backwaters, the coast remains a source of sensations close to paradisial. You can stride along the great spray-misted beaches, delighting in the hard sand nearest the sea; the sea rumbling in higher now and then, taking you unawares; the stones that are perfectly shaped for skipping, so that you feel bound to pick them up and skip them; the objects you find and have to carry home—a shell; a piece of lobster-pot warp; a mustard bottle, scrubbed clean by the sea. Some people sit or lie stunned by the sun and ozone-rich air; others are actively surf-casting, wind-surfing, throwing Frisbees. Children hunt under the rocks for crabs and scream at the sight of jellyfish. On the long stretch of barrier beach guarding Pleasant Bay, Chatham, at the elbow of the Cape, I learnt to swim one summer as a child, wading into deeper and deeper pools of sunwarmed water. On a beach we co-exist with gulls and terns, clams and horse-shoe crabs, the multiple hints of earlier creation.

The water's pull is felt in cities, too. Although lacking the apparent beauty of a National Seashore, the sometimes decrepit wharfs and bulkheaded rip-rap in parts of Boston or Fall River provide places to be in contact with water, perhaps with fishing line in hand. This is the 'Bay State', and an effigy of a cod hangs in the State House on Beacon Hill in Boston. The fish of this coast make a maritime litany: alewife, bass, bluefish, bonito, butterfish, carp, catfish, cod, cunner, cusk, eel, flounder, haddock, hake, halibut, herring, kingfish, mackerel, marlin, perch, pickerel, pollock, salmon, scup, shad, skate, smelt, squid, sturgeon, swordfish, tautog, trout, tuna, turbot, whiting and weakfish. And of course clams, lobsters, oysters and scallops. They furnish the daily quest for the skiffs, lobsterboats and draggers that unload at finger-piers and ramshackle sheds and up-to-date packing houses in coves and harbors. Scrod, a small cod, may be the Boston favorite, but bluefish is mine—preferably broiled over charcoal, with corn that is young and white, and small, freshly-dug potatoes. And blueberries to follow. The native food of this coast is a proper subject for thanksgiving.

This train of thought leads naturally to the large indigenous fowl sacrificed for the last Thursday in November, and to the local berry that accompanies it—these days the cranberry bogs are cultivated with the right depth of peat over sand, and the precise amount of flooding; sun and ocean spray are slightly less determinable. Other parts of the coast are covered with bayberry and beach plum, pitch pine and scrub oak. Beach grass and flowers like Dusty Miller and Beach Pea grow on the long slopes of dunes that face the prevailing wind, but despite this the dunes move—as do the beaches themselves and the inlets through them. (Poison ivy persists!) The tide rises and falls about ten feet north of the Cape, two feet south of it; the water is a good deal cooler once north of the Cape. This produces zones with differing species. North or south, the coast is rich in salt marshes—and I can think of few things I enjoy more than sailing a small boat along a creek winding into such marshes, like those that spread westwards from Plum Island Sound, north of Ipswich, sailing close to the clumps and miniature islands of grass and compacted mud. In these the fiddler crabs find their food and burrow their homes. Clam shells decorate the bottom of the creek. Some intricate inlets lead to large, secluded, kettle-bottomed ponds and some, with shoals as sentries, take us into increasingly narrow confines—like the Pamet River, near Truro on the Cape, which the *Mayflower*'s crew explored during their first bemused month on these shores, in December 1620.

Sometimes, after an afternoon spent bashing wetly into a smoky south-wester in Buzzards Bay or creeping through thick fog in Vineyard Sound, I feel especially grateful for the ponds that afford the best havens, where—safely anchored—we will have for com-

pany a few shellfishermen, a few like-minded sailors, fish jumping, birds flying over. Our gratitude is all the greater because other harbors, in summer, are the nautical equivalent of over-full parking lots; that on Cuttyhunk, the most westerly of the Elizabeth Islands and that on which Gosnold set up his base camp, is often jammed in an unseamanlike way. It only takes the wind to blow harder and change direction in the middle of the night for boats to start banging against each other, with owners shouting, their spotlights flailing. There is generally a dock in such places where you can buy fish and ice and where a boy, minding the dock, will direct you to the nearest grocery store; now and then a healthy trek ensues. The coast provides summer jobs: waitressing; acting as helper on sports-fishing boats; parking cars at big parties; teaching small children how to sail and swim; being a guide or groundskeeper at historic sites and houses.

Here, after all, North American architecture displays its best New England character—whether in austere, ship's-carpentered wood or in elegant, well-bred brick; in granite, steel and glass. Here are the simple white salt boxes of Cape Cod (you can see why Edward Hopper said that all that he wanted to do was paint sunlight striking the sides of houses); the classically inspired Federal and Greek Revival houses in Boston, Newburyport, Salem and Nantucket; the finely proportioned mills and churches and marketplaces (like Faneuil Hall market with its splendidly restored and re-animated arcade); many modern structures, of which a good coastal example may be I.M. Pei's J.F. Kennedy Library, standing starkly black and white, like an up-to-date lighthouse-cum-Coast Guard station, on the infilled Dorchester waterfront overlooking Boston harbor; and in numerous places—like Eastern Point near Gloucester, and Marblehead, Beverly Farms, West Falmouth, Marion, Quisset, and Osterville—the vast shingled houses whose charm now often lies in their butlers' pantries and former servants' bedrooms high under the dormers. Some old summer-houses continue to create a spell that comes perhaps from good times had within them.

Here, too, are the ultimate homes of the late inhabitants of this coast. The graveyards that house them are sadly sweet to wander in, to find—as Nathaniel Hawthorne did on Martha's Vineyard—such stone-cut epitaphs as that (c. 1771) to the Claghornes, a young sailor who drowned, and his wife, who died in childbed:

> John and Lydia, that lovely pair,
> A whale killed him, her body lies here;
> Their souls, we hope, with Christ shall reign—
> So our great loss is their great gain.

Or in the Quaker graveyard on Nantucket, which inspired Robert Lowell's poem to his cousin Warren Winslow:

> Whenever winds are moving and their breath
> Heaves at the roped-in bulwarks of this pier . . .

(I noticed that in the little Quaker cemetery in West Falmouth the headstones were all of the same shape and size, as if to demonstrate the equality of death.)

Other stones, other poems. The Dry Salvages are a group of rocks off Cape Ann, whose name—as T.S. Eliot noted in that section of his 'Four Quartets'—came presumably from the French *les trois sauvages*. Not far away, towards Magnolia and Manchester, is the reef of Norman's Woe, which provided the final destination for the schooner *Hesperus* in Longfellow's poem. It is a coast of distinguished literature—starting, conceivably, with the Icelandic sagas, and going on through Hawthorne's *House of the Seven Gables*, with its secret staircase still to be seen in Salem; Melville's *Moby Dick*, whose whaling men worshipped in the Seamen's Bethel in New Bedford; Kipling's *Captains Courageous*, who sailed out of Gloucester; and John Updike's contemporary citizenry, the couples and commuters of 'Tarbox', whose resemblance to Ipswich has been remarked. And it is hard to think of a patch of New World ground of equivalent size and population that has inspired such writing as

Cape Cod; it would be invidious to list some of the many writers who have lived on it and written about it. Perhaps best to say that the essential text remains Thoreau's account of his three mid-19th century walking tours, entitled simply 'Cape Cod'.

The coast has attracted an equally exalted pantheon of artists: Winslow Homer, Thomas Eakins, Albert Ryder, Fitz Hugh Lane, William Bradford, and of course Edward Hopper, among them. Hopper painted the swell that runs in beside sandspits; the light and shadow on sails—as well as on the sides of houses, the turrets of lighthouses, the flanks of dunes; the telegraph and telephone poles that tilt and loom in the tight streets of coastal towns; and the ledges of rock that line coves. He painted porches and the long straw-colored summer grass that grows around red-brick foundations. In his paintings the light, like Constable's, seems to tell us the time of day.

A coast is also the departures taken from it—lifting off, for example, from Logan over the drumlin islands in Boston harbor, or steaming out of the same harbor after an unexpected visit on the liner *France* (en route from New York to Europe), heading out on a foggy November night across Massachusetts Bay with the ship's horn booming, booming. Or, more recently, sailing out of Menemsha westwards at the end of summer, with a wind on the nose that apparently wanted to keep us there. The seamark and guardian of these waters is the skeletal light tower at the entrance to Buzzard's Bay, whose flashing signal—the chart tells me—can be seen for sixteen miles. On each departure I think of those bits of the coast I mean to explore, and re-explore, when I return.

London, January, 1984   ANTHONY BAILEY

1 Marconi Beach, Cape Cod National Seashore; this beach was named for Guglielmo Marconi, who set up a transatlantic wireless station in the dunes here and sent a radio message to Europe on 19 January 1901. The station operated until 1917 but has been mostly destroyed by erosion.

2 Plum Island has a marvellous beach, five miles long, with 4650 acres of dunes and marshes. It forms part of the Parker River National Wildlife Refuge, a stopover point for birds migrating along the Atlantic Flyway.

3 *(right)* Gay Head, Martha's Vineyard; eroded cliffs of striated, fossil-bearing layers of clay and gravel, 100 million years old. The clay is used in pottery by the local Wampanoag Indians. (Other Massachusetts coastal Indians are the Mashpees, on Cape Cod.) Martha's Vineyard was so named in 1602 by Bartholomew Gosnold after his daughter Martha and the abundant wild grapes which grew there then.

4 *(left)* Dunes at Race Point, at the tip of Cape Cod, that are slowly migrating as a result of wind erosion and the deposition of more sand.

5 'Plimoth Plantation'—a reproduction of the village of the first settlers as it may have been in 1627, four miles from where the original settlement actually stood in what is now downtown Plymouth.

6 Eighteenth century windmill, Brewster.

7 *(right)* Jenny Grist Mill, Plymouth.

8 Unitarian-Universalist Church, Brewster.

9 *(right)* Ancestors of today's New England lie in this graveyard at Newburyport.

10 *(left)* The red brick Custom House, Salem, was built in 1819 and is now part of the Salem Maritime National Historic Site.

11 Shining in the dawn light, a gilded statue of a Bald Eagle watches over Derby Street from Salem's historic Custom House.

12 Moonrise over the National Fore-
fathers Monument, Plymouth; the
topmost statue, of Faith, is 36 feet tall.

13 *(right)* Autumn leaves around the
windows of the library at Manchester, a
snug, hilly town at the southwest end of
the Cape Ann peninsula.

14 The Whaling Museum, New Bedford, on historic Johnny Cake Hill, houses the world's finest collection of scrimshaw and other relics of the whaling era. New Bedford still makes a living from fishing today.

15 (right) This columned shrine surrounds 'Plymouth Rock', a granite boulder that is traditionally regarded as the rock on which the passengers of the Mayflower stepped ashore.

16 The Salem Witch Museum gives audio-visual renderings of the hysterical witch-hunt of 1692, that resulted in the deaths of nineteen people. The statue outside is of Roger Conant, founder of Salem, 1626.

17 *(right)* Winter sunrise lights up the windows of the 'House of Seven Gables' (built in 1668 and restored 300 years later), Salem where Nathaniel Hawthorne's cousin lived and where he visited as a boy. This house is believed to have been the model for the ancestral home of Hawthorne's novel of that name.

18 *(left)* Daffodils by a pond at Beetlebung Corner, Martha's Vineyard.

19 Marblehead, sometimes called 'the yachting capital of the world', is a prosperous seaport which has become a wealthy yachting town; the home of the late L. Francis Herreshoff and the sailmaker Ted Hood.

20 Rockport Harbour reflected in a window at Bearskin Neck.

21 *(right)* Sunrise over some small boat docks, Martha's Vineyard.

22 The modern Boston skyline seen from Swampscott Beach, which was known in the nineteenth century for its small, round-bowed beach dories.

23 Oyster fishing in mid-winter near Wellfleet, Cape Cod; Wellfleet has a
fine expanse of sheltered water, lying as it does behind the protecting hook
of Great Island.

24 'The Hub', Boston; a billboard lights up the night sky above a street festival in Boston's North End.

25 Quincy Market, heart of the revitalized Faneuil Hall marketplace, offers a variety of delicacies, specialty shops, street musicians, acrobats and entertainers.

26 *(left)* Cape Cod Melody Tent, Hyannis, as the audience enters prior to one of the many famous performances.

27 Musicians prepare for an evening performance in the bandstand at Harwich, Cape Cod; the red of their uniforms well suits a place that is known for its cranberries.

28 The Old Town Hall, Salem, overlooks shops and outdoor cafés in Derby Square. The name 'Salem' came from the Hebrew, 'Sholom', meaning 'Peace'—though intolerance was more the word for Salem in the 1690s. The town is historically important in many other respects however, notably for the China trade, as a harbor for pirates, and for its handsome architecture.

29 The Peabody Museum of Salem began with the formation of the East
India Marine Society in 1799 and is the oldest continuously operating
museum in America. The Museum has a fine collection of marine paintings, including many by the talented Roux family, ships' portraitists of
Marseilles. Shown here is the magnificent East India Marine Hall.

30 (left) The Old Granary Burying Ground, Boston, final resting place for many famous early Americans, including John Hancock, Robert Paine, Peter Faneuil, the victims of the Boston Massacre, Samuel Adams and Paul Revere.

31 Interior of the Old North Church (1723) on Salem Street, Boston. This church owed the inspiration of its design to the works of Sir Christopher Wren. The present steeple dates only from 1954 but it was in the steeple of this church, on the night of 11 April 1775, that Paul Revere ordered two lanterns lit ('two if by sea') to give warning that the British were crossing the Charles to Cambridge, shortening their march to Concord. The church bells are those rung by Revere as a boy. The Old North is today the oldest church in Boston.

32 The second floor of Faneuil ('Fan'l') Hall has been a meeting place since
Peter Faneuil gave the building to the city in 1742. From 1763 onwards it
was the principal place where the Colonists met to discuss their griev-
ances, so much so that Sam Adams called it 'The Cradle of Liberty'.

33 The Mariner's Home, founded in 1830 by the Port Society of New
Bedford, where for a small fee a fisherman could be sure of a night's
lodging. The big years of whaling at New Bedford were 1830–60; after the
discovery of oil in Pennsylvania in 1859 the demand for whale oil
declined.

34 Faneuil Hall Marketplace, Boston, a major achievement of restoration and urban revitalization.

35 *(right)* The U.S.S. *Constitution* in Charlestown Navy Yard. A 44-gun frigate, she was built in 1797 and became a veteran of the War against the Barbary States and of the War of 1812 in which she got the nickname 'Old Ironsides'. She is the oldest commissioned ship in the U.S. Navy.

36 (left) Newbury Street runs through Back Bay, one of many parts of Boston reclaimed from the harbour and the rivers, fill being taken, for example, by slicing into the top of Beacon Hill.

37 Nathaniel Hawthorne (1804–64) was born in Salem and there wrote his greatest novel, The *Scarlet Letter* (1850). Salem forms the background for much of his work.

38 Feast of St Anthony, the North End, Boston.

39 *(right)* Sailing enthusiasts attend a boat show on Boston's revitalized waterfront.

40 The Old State House, Boston, was built in 1713 by the British colonial government but after the Revolution was taken over by the Commonwealth of Massachusetts. From its balcony on 18 July 1776 the Declaration of Independence was first read to the citizens of Boston.

41 Brick mansions on cobblestone streets recall the wealth of Nantucket
in its heyday of whaling and shipping.

42 *(left)* King Caesar House, Duxbury, was built in 1807 by Ezra Weston II, a shipbuilder whose great wealth had won him the nickname of 'King Caesar'.

43 Vineyard Haven, main ferry port of Martha's Vineyard for passengers from Woods Hole, quietly awaits the arrival of summer visitors.

44 A tranquil pond near Scituate.

45 *(right)* Dexter Grist Mill, Sandwich, Cape Cod.

46 Entrance to St Peter's Episcopal Church, Buzzard's Bay, Cape Cod.

47 *(right)* Store fronts in Falmouth, Cape Cod.

48 Highland light, Truro, one of the most powerful on the Atlantic coast.
Built in 1797, this was the first light on Cape Cod.

49 Draggers heading into Woods Hole, where the tidal current runs fiercely through the cut between Cape Cod and the Elizabeth Islands, joining Vineyard Sound and Buzzards Bay.

50 The Seaman's Bethel, New Bedford, was described by Herman Melville in *Moby Dick* as the place where sailors prayed before setting sail. Seamen still worship there today.

51 *(right)* Menemsha Basin—tiny, but the chief port of Martha's Vineyard for shellfishermen, sportsfishermen, and lobstermen. The sheds on the crowded waterfront offer a fine selection of freshly caught seafoods. Here a display of tuna tails decorates the side of a hut.

52 First Parish Church on the Common, Cohasset.

53 Cohasset Harbor, mid-winter.

54 Fisherman readying his gear,
Scituate Harbor.

55 *(right)* Annisquam, a late afternoon
in February.

56 Newburyport on the Merrimack River; at one time this beautiful little town was one of the most prosperous in all New England. Some of the finest clipper ships were built here.

57 Downtown Newburyport, after a snowstorm.

58 *(left)* Early morning reflections in a pond at Sandwich, Cape Cod.

59 School House Museum, Eastham, Cape Cod. The arch is made from the jawbone of a whale.

60 *(left)* Gloucester fishing boats with drying nets. Gloucester has been a major fishing center since 1632 and has contributed much to the fishing industry. It is still a big port with a fleet of several hundred boats.

61 Repairing nets on the wharf at Gloucester.

62 Sun-bleached fences to hold in place the massive dunes at Race Point, Cape Cod.

63 (right) Surfers return as fog rolls in on Nauset Beach, Cape Cod.

64 *(left)* Summer afternoon on the beach at Wellfleet.

65 Highland Coast Guard Beach on the National Seashore, Truro, Cape Cod.

66 *(left)* Harvesting cranberries in a flooded bog near Plymouth, which has the headquarters of the cranberry-growers' cooperative, Ocean Spray.

67 Surfcasting for striped bass on the Atlantic shore of Race Point, Cape Cod.

68 Parker River National Wildlife Refuge near Newburyport.

69 Nantucket Harbor, home to the famous old whaling fleets. 'Nantucket' is an Indian word meaning 'distant land'; the island is 30 miles south of Cape Cod. Nantucket's fine harbor and skilled seamen made it the capital of the whaling industry in the early nineteenth century—but it lost its pre-eminence to New Bedford as whaling ships got larger.

70 Pilgrim Hall Museum, Plymouth, dating back to 1824, is the oldest museum in the country. Exhibits of early pilgrim artefacts and paintings are displayed, including the cradle of Peregrine White, born on the *Mayflower*, and Gov. Bradford's Bible.

71 *(right)* Plymouth.

WORK AREA
EMPLOYEES ONLY

72 *(left)* Chatham Fish Pier on Aunt Lydia's Cove, Cape Cod.

73 Nantucket Artists Association, a sign of Nantucket's thriving artistic community.

74 Craggy shores along Pigeon Cove, Cape Ann.

75 *(right)* Wooden bridge to Duxbury Beach, seen from the beach.

76 Brant Rock Beach, near Marshfield.

77 *(right)* This unusually painted fishing boat catches everyone's attention as it docks in Provincetown, Cape Cod.

78 *(left)* West Dennis, Cape Cod.

79 Nauset Light, near Eastham, Cape Cod; built overlooking the cliffs where the 'Three Sisters' lights were long ago lost to erosion. This was a dangerous shore in earlier centuries, especially in easterly gales.

80 *(left)* Low tide on Magnolia's rocky shoreline. Magnolia is a fishing village turned summer resort, turned year-round community.

81 Twilight in old Nantucket.

82 Early morning in Rockport Harbor.

83 Oyster fisherman, Wellfleet.

84 *(left)* Fishing boat heads out to sea as the sun rises on Martha's Vineyard.

85 Winter sunrise, Plymouth Harbor. According to Henry F. Howe,

Prologue to New England (Farrar & Rinehart, 1943) Plymouth was so named since 1614, when Captain John Smith mapped the coast. He spelt it Plimoth. The 102 passengers of the *Mayflower* who arrived in December 1620 seem to have been unaware of Smith's prior visit.

86 Sometimes in summer Marblehead has as many as 2,000 boats moored in the harbor.

87 *(right)* Sunset at Gay Head, Martha's Vineyard.

88 Dawn over Thatcher Island lights off Cape Ann.